D0722904

Countries Around the World

India

Ali Brownlie Bojang

Chicago, Illinois

www.heinemannraintree.com
Visit our website to find out
more information about
Heinemann-Raintree books.

To order:

☎ Phone 888-454-2279

⌨ Visit www.heinemannraintree.com
to browse our catalog and order online.

Edited by Louise Galpine
Designed by Richard Parker
Original illustrations © Capstone Global Library, Ltd.
Illustrated by ODI
Picture research by Mica Brancic
Originated by © Capstone Global Library, Ltd.
Printed by China Translation and Printing Company

16 15 14 13 12
11 10 9 8 7 6 5 4 3 2

Library of Congress Cataloging-in-Publication Data
Brownlie Bojang, Ali, 1949-
  India / Ali Brownlie Bojang.
    p. cm.—(Countries around the world)
  Includes bibliographical references and index.
  ISBN 978-1-4329-5207-5 (hc)
  ISBN 978-1-4329-5232-7 (pb)
1. India—Juvenile literature. I. Title.
DS407.B74 2012
954—dc22   2010038523

Acknowledgments

The author and publisher are grateful to the following for
permission to reproduce copyright material: Alamy pp. 25 (©
Joep Clason), 26 (© Friedrich Stark), 27 (© Penny Tweedie), 29
(© Idris Ahmed); AP/Press Association Images pp. 7 (Rajesh
Kumar Singh), 21 bottom (Saurabh Das), 22 (Gurinder Osan),
23 (Gautam Singh), 32 (Aijaz Rahi), 33 (Eranga Jayawardena),
39 (Prashant Ravi); Getty Images pp. 9 (Hulton Archive/
Central Press), 14 (AFP Photo/Noah Seelam), 17 (Riser/
Manoj Shah), 18 (Photographer's Choice/James Warwick); PA
Archive/Press Association Images p. 21 top; Press Association
Images p. 10 (Topham Picturepoint); Shutterstock pp. 5 (©
Alex Garaev), 6 (© Erick N), 13 (© Galyna Andrushko), 15 (©
Aleksandar Todorovic), 19 (© AJP), 30 (© Edd Westmacott),
31 (© Dirk Ott), 35 (© Absolute-India), 37 (© De Visu), 46 (©
Andrew Chin).

Cover photograph of making offerings to the lake Pichola
during a holy day, Gangaur Ghat, Udaipur, Rajasthan, India,
reproduced with permission of Photolibrary/Age fotostock/©
Alvaro Leiva.

We would like to thank Lawrence Saez for his invaluable help
in the preparation of this book.

Contents

Some words are printed in bold, **like this**. You can find out what they mean by looking in the glossary.

Introducing India

What images come to your mind when someone mentions the word *India*? You may imagine streets packed with women dressed in brightly colored **saris**. You may think of **turbans** or elephants. You will certainly find these in India. But you will find much more as well.

Changing India

There are more poor people in India than in the 26 poorest African countries put together. But India is also one of the fastest-developing countries in the world. As it grows richer, India will likely become more powerful and influential.

India has a population of more than one billion people. Many of them have joined the **middle class** in the past 20 years. It is estimated that there are now about 200 million people in India's middle class. They are able to buy cars, furniture, and clothes. But for most Indians, particularly those who live in small villages in the countryside, life has changed little in recent years. They are still very poor.

Modern cities

The main changes have happened in India's cities, where 30 percent of the people live. In the cities, there are grand, modern hotels, air-conditioned shopping malls, and some of the best restaurants in the world. People in India's cities have lifestyles similar to those of people in many wealthy countries.

How to say...

The name *India* comes from the Indus River. The Hindi word for India is *Bharat*. Both *India* and *Bharat* are official names for India.

Because of its dramatic cliffs and beaches, Kerala, a state in south west India, is a popular tourist destination.

History: A Nation of Nations

Indians are descended from the many different people who have settled in the region over the last 5,000 years. They came from what are today Turkey, Afghanistan, Iran, Greece, and elsewhere. Each group brought its own way of life, but the new arrivals also adapted to the life they found in India. This has resulted in a **multicultural** and **multiethnic** India.

Civilizations and kingdoms

The earliest Indian **civilization** developed in the Indus Valley nearly 5,000 years ago. These people were among the first to build towns. They also farmed and traded. Different kingdoms were established in India. The Gupta **dynasty** ruled northern India nearly 2,000 years ago. The **Mughal** dynasty was founded by **Muslims** who were probably originally from Afghanistan. The Mughals ruled India in the 16th and 17th centuries.

The *Taj Mahal* mausoleum in Agra is entirely covered in white marble.

The waters of the Ganges river are considered to be holy by Hindus. Pilgrims come from all over India to bathe in the river at Varanasi.

The birthplace of religions

Hinduism and **Buddhism**, two important world religions, began in India. Nobody knows how old Hinduism is, but it might date back 6,000 years. Buddhism started about 2,500 years ago, when people began to follow the teachings of a man called Siddhartha Gautama, who was known as the Buddha. Buddhism spread throughout Asia because it was a popular religion with traders who traveled to various parts of Asia.

SHAH JAHAN (1592-1666)

Shah Jahan was a member of the Mughal dynasty. When his wife, Mumtaz Mahal, died, he was so upset he built a huge **mausoleum** in her memory. It took 22 years to build the mausoleum, known as the *Taj Mahal*. It is considered one of the most beautiful buildings in the world.

The arrival of Europeans

Europeans arrived in India in the 15th century. The first to arrive were traders, who bought spices such as cinnamon and cloves and sold them in Europe. At the time, these spices were as valuable as gold. A trading company called the British East India Company began to control parts of India. The company recruited Indians to be soldiers in its own army.

The Indian rebellion

In 1857, the Indian soldiers **rebelled**. They thought the company had too much power. They had also learned that pig and cow fat were being used to oil their rifles. Hinduism forbids the use of cow products, and Islam forbids the use of pig products. This insult to parts of their religions sparked a rebellion. The British army took control from the British East India Company. India became part of the growing British **Empire**.

Independence

Indians wanted to run their own country. During the early 20th century, many Indians began to campaign for **home rule**. Britain gave way to the pressure for independence in 1947, after India helped during World War II. Jawaharlal Nehru became the first prime minister of India. He played an important role in shaping modern India. Indian children still know him as *Chacha* Nehru (Uncle Nehru).

MOHANDAS GANDHI (1869-1948)

Mohandas Gandhi led nonviolent protests against British rule. For example, he encouraged people to **boycott** British goods. He was widely respected, and people called him *Mahatma* (great soul). Gandhi was **assassinated** in 1948 by a Hindu man who thought Gandhi favored Muslims.

Close friends Mohandas Gandhi and Jawaharlal Nehru meet in Bombay (now called Mumbai) in 1946.

Trains were often extremely overcrowded as refugees moved across the Indo-Pakistani border in 1947.

Partition

Before independence, Muslims were a minority in India. They were worried about being ruled by Hindus, who were in the majority. Muslims campaigned for a separate state. Britain and India agreed, and the country of Pakistan was created and separated from India in 1947. This break was known as Partition.

Unfortunately, Partition was not well planned. More than 13 million people traveled across the new border in one direction or the other. Muslims went to Pakistan, and Hindus to India. People were angry at losing their homes and land. It is estimated that as many as one million people died in attacks based on their religion or from exhaustion and hunger on their journeys.

INDIRA GANDHI
(1917-1984)

In 1966, Indira Gandhi, the daughter of Nehru Gandhi, became India's first female prime minister. (She was not related to Mohandas Gandhi.) She was assassinated in 1984 by two of her bodyguards.

India and Pakistan

Tensions still exist between Pakistan and India, particularly over the area of Kashmir, which both countries claim. Since independence, the countries have fought three wars. Both have developed **nuclear weapons** and have threatened each other with them. Relations between the two countries had been improving, but in 2008 a group of Pakistani-based **militants** attacked the Indian city of Mumbai, killing 174 people.

How to say...

A number of Hindi words have become common in the English language, including: bangle, chutney, juggernaut, jungle, loot, pajamas, shampoo, thug, veranda, caravan, and bungalow.

Regions and Resources: Variety and Contrast

India is a triangular-shaped **peninsula** with the Himalayan mountain range to the north, the Arabian Sea to the west, the Bay of Bengal to the east, and the Indian Ocean to the south. India has every kind of landscape and climate you can imagine.

The Himalayas

The Himalayas are the highest mountains in the world, and extend for about 2,500 kilometers (1,550 miles) from west to east. The highest mountain in India is the Kanchenjunga at 8,598 meters (28,208 feet). It is the third-highest mountain in the world.

The Indian landscape includes flat plains, river valleys, desert land, and mountains. Some areas in this map are claimed by India but are under Pakistani or Chinese control.

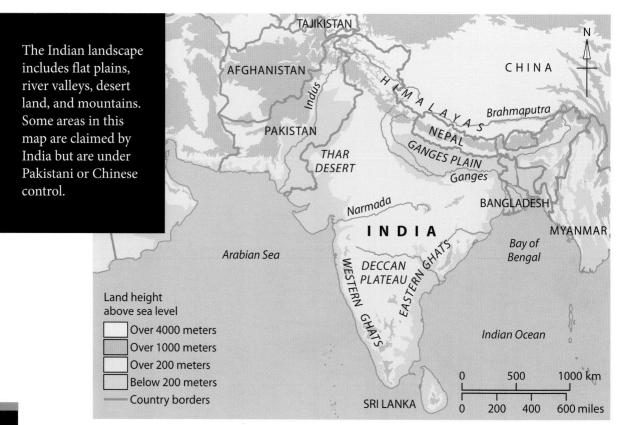

TAJIKISTAN

AFGHANISTAN

CHINA

Indus

HIMALAYAS

Brahmaputra

PAKISTAN

NEPAL

GANGES PLAIN

THAR DESERT

Ganges

Narmada

BANGLADESH

INDIA

MYANMAR

Arabian Sea

DECCAN PLATEAU

WESTERN GHATS

EASTERN GHATS

Bay of Bengal

Indian Ocean

Land height above sea level

Over 4000 meters
Over 1000 meters
Over 200 meters
Below 200 meters
Country borders

SRI LANKA

0   500   1000 km

0   200   400   600 miles

N

Hiking in the Himalayan mountains is a popular tourist activity that helps support the region's local economy.

The Indo-Gangetic Plain

The Indus, the Ganges, and the Brahmaputra rivers carry fertile soil south from the Himalayas and deposit it on the vast, flat Indo-Gangetic Plain. The plain is among the world's great farming regions, producing rice, wheat, sugarcane, and cotton. It is also one of the world's most populated areas, with about one eighth of the planet's population.

The Thar desert

The Thar desert, in the northwest, is an inhospitable area of sand dunes and rocks. In the winter, temperatures fall below freezing, but in the summer they can reach more than 50° Celsius (122° Fahrenheit). The few people that live there are **nomadic**. They move from place to place with their herds of goats or sheep.

YOUNG PEOPLE

Children living in the Thar desert have many jobs to do. They look after goats, sheep, and cows, and collect firewood. School lessons sometimes take place under a tree, but many young people in the Thar travel around too much to go to school.

The Deccan Plateau

The Deccan Plateau, an area of gently rolling hills, covers most of southern India. It is bound by mountain ranges called the Western and Eastern Ghats.

India's varied climate produces weather ranging from heavy rainstorms to devastating **droughts**. Some areas in this map are claimed by India but are under Pakistani or Chinese control.

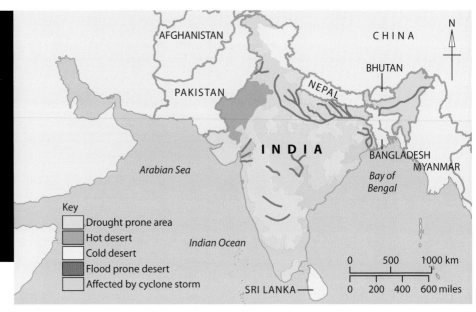

Key
- Drought prone area
- Hot desert
- Cold desert
- Flood prone desert
- Affected by cyclone storm

AFGHANISTAN

CHINA

BHUTAN

PAKISTAN

NEPAL

INDIA

Arabian Sea

BANGLADESH

MYANMAR

Bay of Bengal

Indian Ocean

SRI LANKA

N

0   500   1000 km

0   200   400   600 miles

Climate

India's climate is influenced by **monsoon** rains. The rains are brought by the winds from the southwest. They arrive in southern India towards the end of May and move northwards until by July they affect the whole country. The rains have usually finished by the end of November. The monsoon rains are often heavy and can cause serious flooding. Yet when they fail to come, India sometimes suffers from droughts.

The monsoon rains in 201
were particularly heavy an
caused a lot of flooding.

Resources

India is rich in natural resources. It has minerals such as coal, which is burnt to produce electricity. Burning coal causes **pollution**, however, so new ways of providing electricity for India's huge population need to be found.

India also has iron ore and manganese, which are used to make steel. Other resources found in India include: bauxite, used in the manufacture of aluminum; titanium ore, a metal used in the manufacture of jet engines; natural gas; diamonds; and limestone. Although India produces oil, it cannot keep up with the increasing demand, so it has to import (bring in) oil from Saudi Arabia and the Persian Gulf.

Tea is another product of India. Once picked, tea leaves are carried in large bundles on workers' heads.

Wildlife: From Butterflies to Elephants

India's varied land is home to many different kinds of wildlife. About 200 years ago, forests covered most of India. As India developed, the forests were rapidly cleared to make way for farmland, towns, roads, and railways. As a result, many animals lost their **habitat**. Hunting and **poaching** also threaten the animals.

Today, 172 animal species in India are considered to be under threat. These include the Jenkin's shrew, the Ganges shark, the Himalayan wolf, and the Indian vulture. Some species of monkeys, rhinoceroses, dolphins, and turtles are also endangered.

Keeping wildlife safe

Many animals roam freely throughout India, but in order to help protect them the government has created 166 national parks. These are areas where animals and plants are protected. India's national parks include the Great Himalayan National Park, Corbett National Park in Uttar Pradesh, which is a renowned tiger reserve, and Sundarbans National Park in West Bengal. The parks protect the creatures and the land where they live from hunters and development.

Flowering plants

About 15,000 different flowering plants grow in India. The lotus is the national flower of India. In the northeast, wild orchids and marigolds grow. Other common flowers in India include bougainvillea, rose, and jasmine.

Daily life

Cows are considered sacred in the Hindu religion, and Hindus do not eat beef. It is common to see cows wandering freely around city streets in India. Hindus will not harm a cow in any way, even if it is blocking traffic.

Monkeys, such as this Assamese Macaque monkey, are common all over India.

Diverse life

In the deserts of India, snakes and other reptiles are found among the stunted bushes, grasses, and short acacia trees. And in the dense, warm, tropical forests there is a wealth of wildlife, from swallowtail butterflies to Indian ringneck parakeets, from sloths to wild boars.

For many years, hunting tigers was a popular sport in India. Eventually, so many were hunted that few tigers remained. Project Tiger was launched in 1973 to try to save the Indian tiger. India now has 27 protected areas for tigers, and the number of tigers has increased from 2,000 to 4,000. But the tiger is still a highly endangered species.

Kanha Tiger Reserve in Madhya Pradesh is one of the protected areas where tigers are kept safe.

Elephants are often elaborately decorated for religious festivals.

Elephants have long played an important role in Indian life. They are considered holy in the Hindu religion. Many elephants have been **domesticated**. Some are used in ceremonies and festivals, while others work in forests helping to move tree trunks. India has strict laws protecting elephants, but they are not always obeyed. For example, elephants in temples are sometimes chained to one spot all the time, and farmers often shoot elephants that damage their crops.

YOUNG PEOPLE

Domesticated elephants are often looked after by keepers called *mahouts*. *Mahouts* are introduced to baby elephants when they are young boys, and each boy and his elephant grow up together. A strong bond exists between them. Some people believe *mahouts* have special powers because they can control such a large animal.

Infrastructure: What Makes India Work?

A country's infrastructure is the set of systems and services that are needed for everyday life to run properly. The infrastructure includes power and water supplies, transportation and communication systems, schools, and hospitals.

As in other countries, in India the government is responsible for making sure that things run smoothly. India's government is located in the capital city, New Delhi. India is the largest **democracy** in the world. In India, everyone over age 18 is entitled to vote. India has shown how democracy can work in a huge country containing people from many different ethnic groups, who speak many different languages, and are from different religious backgrounds.

India, the largest democracy in the world, is divided into 28 states and 7 union territories. Some areas in this map are claimed by India but are under Pakistani or Chinese control.

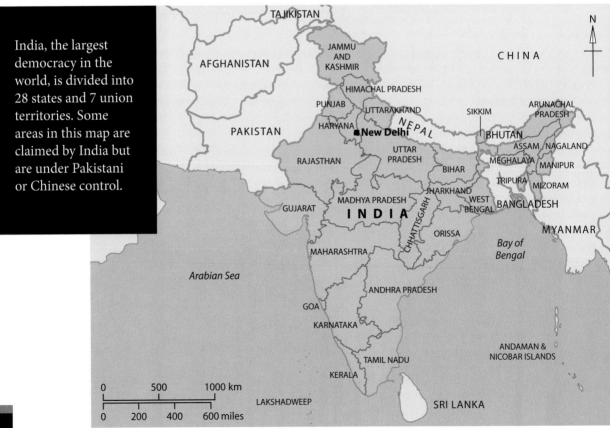

MANMOHAN SINGH

(1932-)

Less than 2 percent of Indians belong to the Sikh religion, so it was notable when Manmohan Singh, a Sikh, became prime minister in 2004. He brought in many economic reforms and tried to help struggling farmers with their debts.

A federation of states

India is split into 28 states and 7 union territories. (Some of the union territories are areas of India that were once French or Portuguese **colonies**.) This system of government is called a **federation**. Each state governs itself to a certain extent and can make rules that apply to the people who live in that state. The state governments mostly deal with concerns such as education and health care. The central government makes decisions that apply across all of India. The central government deals with topics such as industry, defense, and international relations.

In 2009, some voters used electronic voting machines to cast their ballots.

A changing economy

In the 1980s, the Indian government began encouraging foreign companies to establish their businesses in India. It did not put restrictions or high taxes on these companies. Foreign companies were interested because India has a large population of well-educated, English-speaking people.

Booming India

India is now booming. New factories are opening all the time. They make goods such as computers, TVs, washing machines, and cars. The Indian Tata Nano is the world's cheapest car. It costs about $2,500.

India has an important car manufacturing industry. Here a worker tightens the bolt on the engine of a Maruti Swift diesel car.

YOUNG PEOPLE

Suhas Gopinath is 21 years old. When he was 14, he started his own software company, and he now runs a world-class business with 400 employees.

A growing industry in India is the recycling of plastic from old, discarded electrical and electronic equipment.

India's **service industries** are also flourishing. Information technology and **software** development are among the fastest-growing businesses. Many international companies, such as British Airways and American Express, have established call centers in India. Often, if you phone a helpline, you end up talking to someone in India.

The Indian economy is now the fourth-largest in terms of the amount of money people have to spend. Many Indians are better off than they were. Yet at least 200 million Indians remain desperately poor. Many people come to the cities but cannot find work. They end up living in slums or on the streets.

How to say...

The Indian currency is known as the *rupee*. The word comes from the **Sanskrit** word for "silver." The *rupee* is also the currency in Pakistan, Sri Lanka, Nepal, Mauritius, and the Seychelles.

Transportation

India has an extensive railway system, which was built during British rule. When people think of Indian trains, they sometimes imagine overcrowded cars with people sitting on the roof and hanging on to the sides. But, in fact, long distance travel can be luxurious in air-conditioned sleeper cars. Indian railways carry 20 million passengers every day.

One of the biggest problems in India's cities is traffic and the pollution it causes. Public transportation—buses and motorized **rickshaws**—are popular. But more and more people have their own cars, and traffic is often at a standstill. Many people use motorcycles to get around the traffic jams. You often see a family of four on one motorcycle!

Communication

The number of cell phones is growing faster in India than anywhere else in the world. Even in remote villages, many people use cell phones. There are an estimated 564 million cell phones in India. That's almost one cell phone for every two people!

Young people use technology to communicate with each other, through social linking websites and e-mail. Facebook is now available in Hindi, and many young people use Twitter.

Daily life

In Mumbai, most people go to work by train. The trains carry nearly 7 million commuters to and from work every day. During rush hour, the trains are very crowded. People pack into cars so tightly they can hardly breathe!

Riding in a crowded *tuk tuk* is one of the many ways children travel to and from school.

School

All children in India are supposed to go to school from the ages of 6 to 14. School can be anything from an expensive boarding school to a bus that travels from place to place. But not all children go to school. Many poor children have to work. Some go to school at night, after a hard day's work.

There is a big difference between the standards of education in different Indian states. In Kerala, the local government spends a lot of money on schools, and more than 90 percent of adults can read. But in Bihar, less than 50 percent of adults can read. Schools in towns and cities are usually better than those in villages.

In India, children often wear uniforms to school. These children are in a classroom in Tamil Nadu.

YOUNG PEOPLE

Many Indian parents think that school is less important for girls than for boys. While their brothers attend school, many girls stay at home to help with housework. The government is trying to encourage parents to see that education is important for all children.

Mobile health programs help doctors serve people in remote areas. Each mobile unit is like a doctor's office on wheels.

Health care

In India, the quality of health care varies tremendously between the rich and poor. Poor people often get illnesses such as typhoid and dysentery, which spread easily where people do not have clean water. Some villages have small health clinics. Otherwise, villagers rely on occasional visits from a nurse or doctor.

Rich Indians have excellent health care. Some Indian hospitals are so good that people come from Europe and the United States to be treated there.

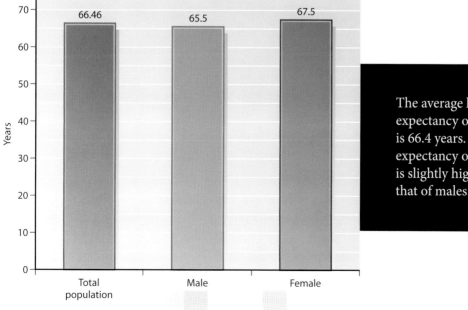

The average life expectancy of Indians is 66.4 years. The life expectancy of females is slightly higher than that of males.

Culture: Tradition and Change

India arose from a mix of peoples from different regions, who brought with them different languages, religions, and cultures.

Religion

Hindus, who make up about 80 percent of the population, worship many different gods. A small room in each house is often kept as a shrine where family members pray to their particular god.

Although only 13.4 percent of Indians are Muslim, the country has the third-largest Muslim population in the world, after Indonesia and Pakistan. Buddhism, Sikhism, Christianity, Jainism, and Judaism are other religions practiced in India.

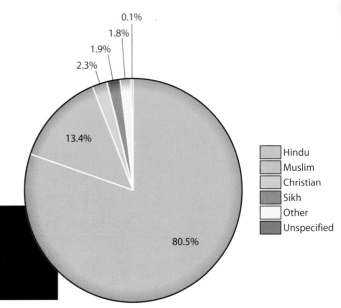

Many different religions are practiced in India. Hinduism, with 80.5 percent of Indians as followers, is the most practiced.

0.1%
1.8%
1.9%
2.3%
13.4%
80.5%

Hindu
Muslim
Christian
Sikh
Other
Unspecified

Daily life

Each Hindu person is born into a **caste**, or class. This often determines the kind of job they have and whom they can marry. The government has outlawed treating people from different castes in a certain way, but unfortunately the caste system is still followed by many Indians.

Brightly colored powder shimmers in the air during the *Holi* festival.

Festivals and holidays

India has many festivals. The main Hindu festivals are *Diwali*, or the festival of lights, and *Holi*, which celebrates the harvest. During *Diwali*, children are given candy, and fireworks fill the sky. During *Holi*, children throw brightly colored powder at each other. It is great fun!

For Sikhs, some of the Hindu festivals are also important. Among the main Muslim festivals is *'Id al-Fitr*, which marks the end of the month of *Ramadan*. During *Ramadan*, Muslims fast from sunrise to sunset.

Some Indian holidays are celebrated only by people of particular religions or those who live in particular areas, but there are three national public holidays: Republic Day on January 26, Independence Day on August 15, and Mahatma Gandhi's birthday on October 2.

Food

Indian food has become popular around the world. It is spicy and tasty and is eaten with either rice or bread, depending on the region. In the north, milk and meat are used in cooking, but in the south coconut is used. Most people in the south are vegetarian.

Broccoli Bajji recipe

Bajjis are a traditional South Indian food. If you like, you can use a different vegetable, such as cauliflower.

Ingredients

- 2 cups gram flour
- 2 tablespoons rice flour
- 2 teaspoons chili powder
- a pinch of baking soda
- salt to taste
- 2 cups broccoli florets
- ½ cup water
- ¼ cup oil for frying

! HOT OIL CAN BURN! Get an adult to help you with this recipe.

Instructions

Mix the two flours with the chili powder, baking soda, and salt. Add water slowly, and mix well to avoid lumps. Heat the oil in a deep frying pan or a wok. When the oil is hot, dunk a piece of broccoli in the batter. Coat it completely and then carefully put it into the hot oil. Fry just a few at a time. When the broccoli is brown remove with a draining spoon and put on a kitchen paper to drain. Enjoy!

In 1996 the city of Bombay had its name officially changed to Mumbai. This is the original Marathi name which comes from the goddess Mumba who was worshipped by the early residents of the area.

Daily life

In cities such as Mumbai, lunch is delivered to office workers by *dabbawallas*, which means "lunch-box deliverers." Wives usually make lunch for their husbands and pack them in metal containers called *tiffins*, which they give to the *dabbawallas* to deliver in time for lunch. The *dabbawallas* then return the *tiffins* to the owners.

TV and film

TV is popular in India. Indians with cable TV can watch foreign channels such as the BBC and CNN. Many Indians like game shows and soap operas. The soap operas are usually based on family life and are dramatic—sometimes overly dramatic!

Many young Indians enjoy going to see a Bollywood film. Bollywood got its name because the films were made in Bombay (now known as Mumbai), so the B in Bombay replaced the H in Hollywood to get Bollywood. More films are made in India than anywhere else in the world—even Hollywood. Most Indian films are musicals. They feature dancing and are full of romance, villains, and action.

Bollywood films are filled with dramatic dance performances and bright colors.

Sport and games

Many games and sports started in India, including chess and polo. Polo is similar to hockey but is played on horseback. India has won eight gold medals in field hockey, the national sport, but cricket is the most popular sport. Indians are passionate about cricket, and good players are as popular as film stars.

Soccer is increasingly popular, and young people are playing more basketball, volleyball, and badminton. In cities, many Indians play tennis. Leander Paes, the leading Indian tennis player, has won many doubles titles.

Indian cricketer, Virender Sehwag, is considered to be one of the top batsmen in the world today.

YOUNG PEOPLE

One of the most popular children's games in India is *dabba ice-pais*, which is a bit like hide-and-seek. Children also play *lagori*, in which each team has to stop the other from building a pile of stones, and *gilli-danda*, in which a large stick is used to hit a smaller stick.

India Today

India is changing rapidly. This presents the country with many challenges that it will need to find ways of dealing with in the near future.

Climate change

Global climate change could have serious effects in India. Higher temperatures could result in stronger **cyclones**, and the monsoon rains could become more unpredictable. This could result in both more flooding and more droughts.

Changing families

Although the idea of family remains important in India, how people live together is changing. A few years ago, many different members of one family lived together— grandparents, nephews and nieces, aunts and uncles. Now more Indians live in cities in small apartments, with just parents and their children.

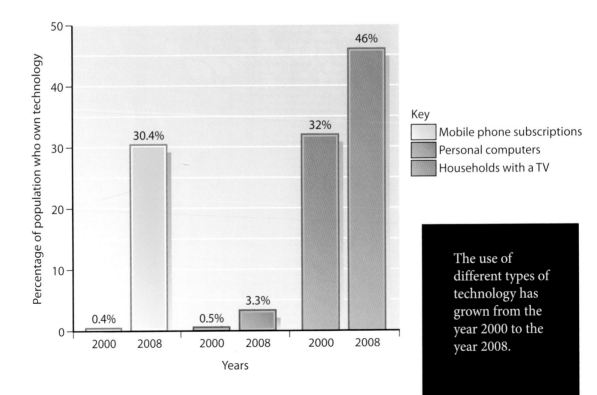

Key
- Mobile phone subscriptions
- Personal computers
- Households with a TV

The use of different types of technology has grown from the year 2000 to the year 2008.

Young people are better educated and more ambitious than their parents. But there is often conflict between parents and children, which would not have been tolerated a few years ago. Until recently, young women were expected to have an **arranged marriage** and take care of their husbands. Now, many young women are going to college and getting jobs. They are more outspoken about what they want from life, including whom they will marry.

Young people in India share many of the same interests and experiences as children in other countries around the world.

A growing population

With nearly 1.2 billion people, India has the second-largest population in the world, following only China. But India's population is growing faster than China's, and it is estimated that in 2045 it will overtake it. India needs to be able to look after this growing population in the future.

Fact File

Official name: Republic of India

Bordering countries: Pakistan, China, Nepal, Bhutan, Bangladesh, and Burma

Area: 3.3 million square kilometers (1.3 million square miles)

Major rivers: Ganges, Brahmaputra, Narmada

Population: 1.18 billion (2010 estimate)

Official languages: Hindi, Bengali, Telugu, Marathi, Tamil, Urdu, Gujarati, Malayalam, Kannada, Oriya, Punjabi, Assamese, Kashmiri, Sindhi, and Sanskrit. English is a subsidiary official language.

Capital city: New Delhi

Largest cities: Mumbai, Delhi, Bangalore, Kolkata, Chennai

Highest point: Mount Kanchenjunga, 8,598 meters (28,208 feet)

Lowest point: Indian Ocean, sea level

Currency: Rupee

Main exports: Petroleum products, precious stones, machinery, iron and steel, chemicals, vehicles, clothes

Main imports: Crude oil, precious stones, machinery, fertilizer, iron and steel, chemicals

Main trading partners: China, the United Arab Emirates, Saudi Arabia, the United States

The face of Mohandas Gandhi is featured on Indian *rupee* bank notes.

Life expectancy: 66.4 years

Major religions: Hindu (80.5%), Muslim (13.4%), Christian (2.3%), Sikh (1.9%), other (1.8%) (2001 census)

Literacy rates: 61% (male 73.4, female 47.8%)

Percentage of population below the poverty line: 25

Fact File

Public holidays: Republic Day January 26, Independence Day August 15, Mahatma Gandhi's birthday October 2

World Health ranking: 112 out of 190 (UK - 18, USA - 37)

Famous Indians: Shahrukh Khan is one of the most famous and influential actors and producers of Indian films in India. Many of his films have been blockbusters.

Arundhati Roy won the Booker Prize in 1997 for her first novel *The God of Small Things*. She is also a social campaigner for homeless and poor people in India.

Salman Rushdie is one of the most famous authors of Indian origin. He won the Booker prize for his book *Midnight's Children*.

Professor Amartya Kumar Sen is one of the greatest intellectuals and economists in the world. He is well known for his ideas about the global economy.

Ravi Shankar made a major contribution towards making Indian music popular in the West. He played an instrument called the *sitar* and had a strong influence on the music of the Beatles.

Bodhgaya in Bihar is where Buddha lived and is the birthplace of Buddhism. The famous statue of the Buddha in Bodhgaya is over 200 years old.

National pride

India's national anthem was written by Rabindranath Tagore and was adopted 1950.

Jana Gana Mana

Thou art the ruler of the minds of all people,
Dispenser of India's destiny.
Thy name rouses the hearts of the Punjab,
Sind, Gujarat, and Maratha,
Of the Dravida, and Orissa and Bengal.
It echoes in the hills of Vindhyas and
Himalayas,
Mingles in the music of the
Jamuna and the Ganges and is chanted by the waves of
the Indian Sea.
They pray for the blessings and sing thy praise.
The saving of all people waits in thy hand,
Thou dispenser of India's destiny.
Victory, victory, victory to thee.

Timeline

BCE means "before the common era." When this appears after a date it refers to the number of years before the Christian religion began. BCE dates are always counted backward.

CE means "common era." When this appears after a date, it refers to the time after the Christian religion began.

BCE

ca. 3000	Civilization develops in the Indus River valley.
ca. 500	Buddhism starts in India.
530	Persians invade India.
325	Alexander the Great invades northern India.
36	The Ancient Greeks invade India.

CE

300s	The Gupta dynasty is founded in northern India.
700s	Muslims arrive in India.
1192	Muslim armies conquer much of northern India.
1192	Muslim general Muhammed Ghor captures Delhi and a dynasty of rulers to last about 200 years starts.
1400s	Europeans begin arriving in India.
1498	Vasco da Gama, a Portuguese explorer, arrives in India.
1526-1857	India ruled by the Mughals—a time of great art and architecture.
1632	Construction begins on the Taj Mahal.
1857	Indian soldiers rebel against the British.

1858	India comes under the rule of the British Empire.
1920	Mahatma Gandhi starts nonviolent protests against British rule.
1947	India gains independence from the UK; India and Pakistan are partitioned.
	India and Pakistan go to war over Kashmir, ending in 1948.
1948	Mahatma Gandhi is assassinated
1965	India and Pakistan go to war for the second time.
1966	Indira Gandhi becomes India's first female prime minister.
1971	India and Pakistan go to war for the third time.
1974	India explodes its first nuclear device under ground.
1975	PM Indira Gandhi declares state of emergency after electoral malpractice.
1992	Violence between Hindus and Muslims erupts, following the demolition of a mosque in Ayodhya.
2000	India marks the birth of its one billionth citizen.
2004	Manmohan Singh becomes India's first Sikh prime minister.
2008	Nearly 200 people are killed in an attack on Mumbai by militants from Pakistan.
2010	The Commonwealth Games are held in New Delhi.

Glossary

arranged marriage marriage in which parents decide whom their children will marry

assassinate murder of an important person such as the leader of a country

boycott organized refusal to use a service or buy a product as a form of protest

Buddhism religion based on the teachings of Siddhartha Gautama

caste position in society that is given to someone at birth

civilization way in which a society organizes itself

colony community settled in a new land but with ties to another government

cyclone violent storm in a tropical area

democracy government system in which people vote for their leaders

domesticated describes an animal that has been tamed

drought period of little or no rainfall

dynasty line of rulers from the same family

empire lands ruled by one country

federation country made up of several states that have some self-government

habitat where an animal naturally lives

Hinduism main religion of India, which includes the worship of many gods

home rule idea that people should govern themselves

illegal against the law

mausoleum large or fancy tomb

middle class social class that includes people who are educated and work in professional jobs

militant person who fights for a cause

monsoon wind in the Indian Ocean and southern Asia that often carries heavy, unpredictable rain

Mughals Muslim rulers of northern India in the 16th and 17th centuries

multicultural relating to several different cultures

multiethnic relating to several different ethnic groups

Muslim person who follows the religion of Islam

nomadic describes someone who travels around with animals rather than settling in one place

nuclear weapon very powerful bomb

peninsula land surrounded by water on three sides

poaching hunting animals illegally

pollution harmful chemicals in the air

rebel refuse to accept authority and/or organize resistance to being governed

rickshaw tricycle used for transporting people

Sanskrit ancient language of India

sari garment worn by Indian women consisting of several yards of materials

service industry area of work in which people perform a service rather than growing food or making products

software programs used in computers

turban piece of thin material wrapped around the head and usually worn by men of the Sikh religion

Find Out More

Books

Cleveland, Rob. *The Drum: A Folktale from India*. Atlanta: August House Publishers, 2006.

Cumming, David. *Country Insights: India*. London: Hodder Wayland, 2006.

Das, Prodeepta. *Geeta's Day: From Dawn to Dusk in an Indian Village*. London: Frances Lincoln, 2003.

Das, Prodeepta. *Prita Goes to India*, London: Frances Lincoln, 2007.

Ganeri, Anita, and Rachel Wright. *India* (Country Topics). New York: Franklin Watts, 2007.

Godard, Philippe. *Kids Around the World: We Live in India*. New York: Abrams, 2006.

Heine, Theresa. *Elephant Dance: A Journey to India*. Cambridge, MA: Barefoot Books, 2006.

Milbourne, Anna, and Linda Edwards. *Stories from India*. London: Usborne, 2004.

Noble, Marty. *Traditional Designs from India*. Mineola, NY: Dover Publications, 2008.

Powell, Jillian. *Looking at Countries: India*. New York: Franklin Watts, 2010.

Rose, Deborah Lee. *The People Who Hugged the Trees: An Environmental Folk Tale*. Lanham, MD: Roberts Rinehart, 2004.

Troughton, Joanna. *The Tiger Child: A Folk Tale from India*. New York: Puffin, 1996.

Websites

www.ancientindia.co.uk/
See artifacts from ancient India at the British Museum website.

www.chembakolli.com/
Videos, slides, and more showing life and change in an Indian village.

www.goingtoschool.com/projects_gsi.html
Short descriptions about children going to school in different parts of India.

http://india.mrdonn.org/gupta.html
Find out more about the Gupta dynasty.

www.oxfam.org.uk/education/resources/clothes_line/?130
A resource exploring cotton production and the textile industry in India for students ages 7 to 11.

http://www.ancientindia.co.uk/
See artifacts from ancient India at the British Museum website.

Places to Visit

Taj Mahal, Agra
http://www.tajmahal.org.uk/

The palaces of Rajasthan
Palaces once lived in by a powerful Hindu caste. Many are now hotels.
http://www.rajasthanpalaces.com/

The Golden Temple in Armritsar
A place of beauty for peace and meditation.
http://sacredsites.com/asia/india/amritsar.html

The Royal Pavilion in Brighton was built in Indian style in about 1815.
http://www.pavilionfoundation.org/

The Museum of Asian Art in Berlin
The largest museum of ancient Asian art in the world.
http://www.smb.museum/smb/sammlungen

The Asian Art Museum in San Francisco
Contains Indian sculptures, paintings, and other forms.
http://www.asianart.org/

Topic Tools

You can use these topic tools for your school projects. Trace the flag and map on to a sheet of paper, using the thick black outlines to guide you, then color in your pictures. Make sure you use the right colors for the flag!

The flag of India was adopted in 1947. The saffron (orange) stands for courage, the white for purity and truth, and the green for faith.

New Delhi

N

Index